Life Cycles
From Tadpole to Frog

Sally Hewitt

QED Publishing

First published in the UK in 2005 by
QED Publishing
A Quarto Group company
226 City Road
London EC1V 2TT
www.qed-publishing.co.uk

A Catalogue record for this book is available from the British Library.

ISBN 1 84538 449 0

Written by Sally Hewitt
Designed by Caroline Grimshaw
Editor Hannah Ray
Picture Researcher Nic Dean

Series Consultant Anne Faundez
Publisher Steve Evans
Creative Director Louise Morley
Editorial Manager Jean Coppendale

Printed and bound in China

Picture credits

Key: t = top, b = bottom, m = middle, l = left, r = right

ardea.com/Ian Beames (LBO) 16, 21t; Corbis/Roger Tidman 4, 18t, 22tl,
/DK Limited 5, /George McCarthy 12, /Chris Newton; Frank Lane Picture
Library 13, /Frank Blackburn; Ecoscene 15, /Pat Jerrold; Papillo 19t;
Ecoscene/Robert Picket 9, 11, 20t, 22t, 22b, /Anthony Cooper 17, 21b;
FLPA/ Foto Natura Stock 7t, 18b, 22mb, /Alwyn J. Roberts 7b;
photolibrary.com/Oxford Scientific 10t, /Michael Leach/OSF 14;
Still Pictures/Hans Pfletschinger 6, 8, 10b, 19b, 22ml.

Contents

Frogspawn

Something is floating on the edge of the pond. It looks like spotty jelly!

It is thousands of tiny frogs' eggs, called **frogspawn**.

Ten days
go by.

The sun
warms the
frogspawn.

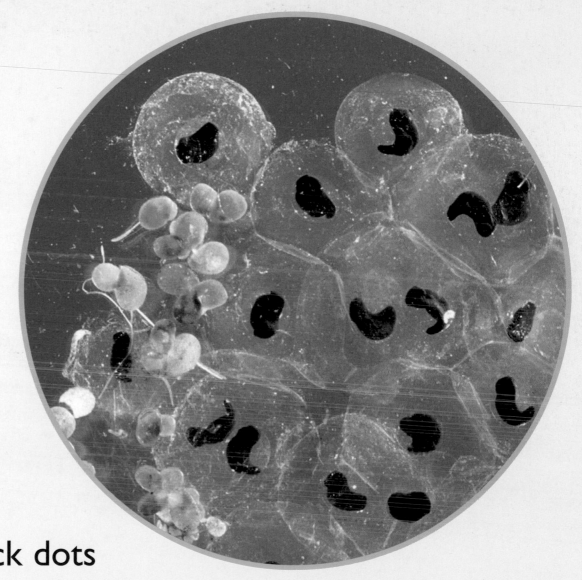

The little black dots
grow bigger and start
to change shape.

Tadpoles

Tiny **tadpoles** wriggle out of the jelly and swim away.

They have big heads and long tails.

The tadpoles eat water plants.

A big fish in the pond watches the little tadpoles. Big fish eat little tadpoles!

Breathing underwater

Young tadpoles stay underwater all the time. They breathe through **gills** on the side of their heads.

But tadpoles keep changing! At four weeks old, they start to breathe through new gills inside their bodies.

Froglets

When they are eight weeks old, the tadpoles grow two back legs. Now, the tadpoles swim to the surface to take gulps of air.

A few weeks later, the tadpoles grow front legs, too.

Then the tadpoles' tails slowly disappear.

The tadpoles have become little frogs called **froglets**.

They have long back legs for hopping and **webbed feet** for swimming.

11

Water and land

Froglets swim
in the pond,
and sit on
stones and
lily leaves.

They hop around on land
and hide in long grass.

12

Foxes and herons hunt for frogs.

But little speckled frogs are hard to spot in the grass.

Frogs

All summer, the little frogs eat
and eat, and grow and grow.
There is plenty of food around.

In autumn, the leaves start to fall from the trees and it begins to get colder.

There is not so much food for the young frogs now.

Winter and spring

The frogs find
a hiding place
in piles of leaves
or under logs.

They sleep
through the
cold winter.

16

Spring comes and the frogs wake up.
The male croaks to attract a female.

Now there is a new clump of frogspawn
on the edge of the pond.

What do you think?

In what part of a pond might you find frogspawn?

Can you remember what tiny tadpoles eat?

Why do bigger tadpoles
swim to the surface
of the pond?

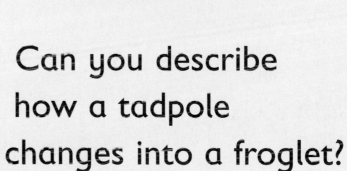

Can you describe
how a tadpole
changes into a froglet?

What helps froglets to hop? What helps them to swim?

How does a frog's skin help it to hide?

Can you remember why frogs go to sleep for the winter?

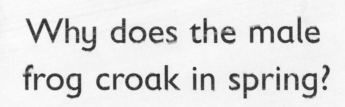

Why does the male frog croak in spring?

Glossary

Froglet – a baby frog that looks just like a grown-up frog.

Frogspawn – a clump of thousands of frogs' eggs. Each egg is a black dot surrounded by jelly.

Gills – the parts of a tadpole's body that are used to breathe underwater.

Tadpoles – small, black, fish-like creatures. As they grow, they change into frogs.

Webbed feet – feet are webbed when the toes are joined together by pieces of skin.

Index

Parents' and teachers' notes

- Look at the cover of the book. Talk about why the picture has been chosen for the cover.
- Read the title together. Discuss what it tells you about the content of the book.
- Explain that this is a non-fiction book, which gives us facts and information. Talk about the difference between fiction, which tells a story, and non-fiction.
- Read the book with your child, discussing the photographs as you read. What extra information do the photographs give the reader?
- Spend time talking about the answers to the questions on pages 18–21. Take the opportunity to look back through the book to check your answers.
- Identify the contents page, the glossary and the index. Talk about why a book needs these pages.
- Using the contents page, look up the page on 'Froglets'.
- Point out that the index is in alphabetical order. Explain that the index tells us where in the book we can find certain information. Use the index to look up the references to 'frogspawn'.

- Find the words in **bold** type and look them up in the glossary.
- Together, talk about the life cycle of a tadpole/frog. Point out that the book ends where it started, with frogspawn.
- Draw a circle. Draw frogspawn, a tadpole, a froglet and a frog around the circle to illustrate the concept of a life cycle. Ask your child to run a finger around the circle, starting and ending with the frogspawn.
- Talk together about all the different stages in the life cycle. Ask your child to describe what the frogspawn, tadpoles, froglets and frogs look like. Talk about their respective size, shape and colour.
- Ask your child to explain the life cycle of a frog to you in his or her own words.
- Talk about how babies are born and grow into adults, and compare the way a tadpole changes as it grows into a frog.
- Talk about camouflage and why it is important for froglets to be difficult to spot.